CHARACTER BUILDING

FOR AFRICAN CENTERED SCHOLARS

GRADES 4 AND UP

Paris,
Thank you!
Love,
Nikala Asante
8/29/15

NIKALA ASANTE

ASANTE EDUCATIONAL WORKS

ISBN-13: 978-1515069546

ISBN-10: 1515069540

Dedicated to all African-centered educators and the children that we serve, globally.

TABLE OF CONTENTS

INTRODUCTION

Firstly, I want to thank you for allowing me to share in your journey towards providing your children with a holistically excellent education. By holistically excellent, I mean that you are shaping your children to not just achieve great academic successes, but to become well-rounded and culturally centered adults.

The many sacrifices that we make to educate our children are for one reason and one reason only - to shape them into successful, critically thinking, and independent adults, with good characters.

Which traits are representative of the ideal adults that we are molding?

Dr. Amos Wilson, author of many books on African American child psychology, such as *The Developmental Psychology of the Black Child* and *Awakening the Natural Genius of Black Children*, offers a list of attributes to cultivate in Black children based on traditional African values[1].

- respect for adults
- independence
- persistence
- curiosity
- experimentation
- discovery
- universal sense of justice
- respect for order
- social interest

---

[1] *Awakening the Natural Genius of Black Children,* Dr. Amos Wilson

- good manners
- sensitivity to persons and environment
- self-esteem/family and community pride
- commitment to promises made or contracts
- love of learning
- ethnic/cultural identity
- general care for humans of all races
- reverence for life

How do we nurture these traits within our children? The first and best way to teach our children any good habit is to model it. Outside of that, whichever spiritual system that we practice will serve as much of the moral foundation for our children. Even if you do not consider yourself religious, be sure to discuss morals on a regular basis. We can also look to the moral guidelines of traditional African societies. We can teach our children to not just memorize them, but to practice them in daily life.

We will examine traditional African principles and guidelines within this book. I will also share fun and interactive methodologies to put them into practice. Thank you again and please visit **blackhomeschoolmom.com** regularly for more great resources and ideas. All the best to you and your family.

Love and Light,

Nikala Asante

Photography Credit:
Dr. Obari Cartman

HOW TO USE THIS BOOK

This book is meant to be utilized in order, from beginning to end. It can be mainly self-guided by the student, with some teacher/parental support. If your student is taking the self-guided approach, please review the lessons, discuss them, and choose one or more of the activities listed at the end of each section for your student to complete after the lesson.

You can also use this book to create your own lesson plans. For example, **Ma'at** can be broken down into lesson plans on each of the Seven Principles of Ma'at. Afterwards, you can have your student to complete a creative activity or community service extension to demonstrate his or her understanding of the principle.

This book is designed for students Grade 4 – Grade 12, a huge range of ages. A gifted 4th grader can use this book successfully, as can any middle school or high school student. If you feel that you need to simplify a lesson or expand it for your student's learning level, please feel free to do so.

There are lined sections included in some chapters so that your student can write directly in the book. You can also designate a special composition book or spiral notebook for any written activities that will not fit in this book.

Also, there is a section titled **My Glossary** in the back of this book. It is a different type of glossary than what your student may have ever experienced before. This glossary is blank – it only contains lines for writing. Whenever your student reaches a word that he or she does not know, have him or her to write the word in the glossary. Then, have your student to look up the word and write the short definition. In this way, **My Glossary** is catered to each individual student. Also, memory retention will be improved.

There is also a section titled **My Notes** in the back of this book with lined pages where your student can note items of interest. When you are assigning work, you can advise your student to take notes in the **My Notes** section or to use it as a tool for reflection after each lesson is done.

You may need to purchase the following materials: poster boards, markers, crayons, paint, fabric markers or fabric paint, blank tee shirts, printer paper, and cardstock paper. Feel free to substitute some of these items with items that you already have at home. For example, your student may have an old solid colored tee shirt to use for one of the art activities – so you do not have to buy a new one.

If you have any questions, please send me a message through **blackhomeschoolmom.com.** I appreciate you allowing me to be a part of this beautiful journey towards helping your child to develop his or her character to its maximum potential of goodness. Thank you.

~ Nikala Asante

CHARACTER BUILDING PRINCIPLES

MA'AT

"I have satisfied God with that which He loves. I have given bread to the hungry, water to the thirsty, clothes to the naked, and a boat to those without one." – *The Book of Coming Forth by Day*

Ma'at is a concept of morality that originated in *Kemet* (ancient Egypt). The figure of Ma'at as expressed in hieroglyphic carvings is that of a woman with extended wings or a woman with a feather on her crown.

According to this spiritual philosophy, when a human being transitions out of the physical realm (death), he or she meets Ma'at, and then his or her heart is weighed against a feather.

If one's heart is weighted heavily with wrongdoing and poor character, it will be eaten by *Ammit*[2], a monstrous being who is part lion, part crocodile, and part hippopotamus. Once this happens, one will not be able to achieve eternal life, but will instead become a restless spirit – a ghost.

[2] By Ammit.svg: Jeff Dahl derivative work: Insider (Ammit.svg) [CC BY-SA 3.0 (http://creativecommons.org/licenses/by-sa/3.0)], via Wikimedia Commons

How do we interpret this in modern day terms? First, let's look at the meaning of eternal life, or immortality. Can one truly become immortal? If so, we have not witnessed this phenomenon on earth. However, we do see that humans have achieved immortality through their legacies.

For example, let's examine the story of Imhotep, who is best known for being the architect of the oldest known pyramid. He was born around 2,667 BCE – nearly 5,000 years ago. Imhotep was born neither rich nor privileged, but he worked hard to develop his intelligence and to be of service to those greater than him. He did not just sit around and think, "I wish that I was smarter," – he studied regularly to build his knowledge. He did not just read to make good grades or to impress others. He put his knowledge into action. In turn, he developed 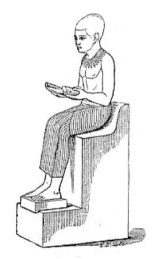 himself into the first known physician, a legendary architect, a brilliant poet, a scribe, an astronomer, and the advisor to King Djoser. He went from being a regular kid with no special head start in life to being a multi-talented genius who gave advice to the *king*. Wow, isn't that incredible?

As a result of Imhotep's practice of good character, he left a legacy that is still widely honored and studied nearly 5,000 years later. That is a form of immortality.

Imagine – what if people are still learning from your life 5,000 years from now? That was the goal of many ancient Egyptians – to live their lives so well, with such upright actions, with such beneficial works, that people would still study their lives as examples for how to live, thousands of years later. Let's now examine the principles of Ma'at to understand how the Kemetic people went about striving towards immortality.

SEVEN PRINCIPLES OF MA'AT

1. Truth
2. Justice
3. Harmony
4. Balance
5. Order
6. Reciprocity
7. Propriety

What do these principles mean and how can we practice them daily?

TRUTH – Truth is to tell what really happened, i.e. not telling lies. But, truth is also to understand what is real and what is false. When we commit to learning history, we can separate fact from fiction and take action based on full knowledge.

For example, we know that Christopher Columbus did not discover America, so we do not honor him, celebrate him, or idolize him in any way. We instead honor and celebrate real leaders who made sincere contributions to the advancement of African people all over the world, and to all humanity.

Truth also applies to being able to critically analyze the information that we receive for flaws or *biases*. If we read a news article that refers to one young male who got into some trouble as a "criminal", and another young male of a different ethnic group or culture who made a similar mistake as a "troubled teen" - that is a bias. They may have both been troubled teens who needed help.

You can then write in to the news outlet asking them to make a correction, or you can write your own newspaper or blog to report from a more unbiased perspective. Actions like these would demonstrate your commitment to truth, and also help shape your legacy.

JUSTICE – Justice is fairness or evenhandedness. Imagine that an awesome dinner has been prepared, with all of your favorite foods. You are super excited about it. You can taste it already.

When the food is served, your friend, who is your same age and same size, is given huge portions of each dish, while you are only given a teaspoon of each dish. Is this fair?

Similarly, certain people, because of their race, class, or culture are consistently paid more than others for doing the same jobs with the same education levels. Is that fair?

If you do a little research on housing, economics, and education, you will see that disparities like this exist all over the world. We should all be entitled to support ourselves in a comparable way in any and every career field.

You can help foster justice at home, at school, and in your community by always speaking up for fair treatment. Nationally and globally, you can attend protests[3] and sign petitions for resources like money and opportunities to be distributed fairly. Also, you can start your own business or businesses,

[3] Visit avaaz.org or change.org to find a petition to sign with your parents today.

employ others, treat them fairly, and pay them fairly.

HARMONY – Harmony is to be in agreement or in accord. If you play a musical instrument, you probably know a lot about harmony. Let's say that you are in a band, playing the instrument of your choosing. Personally, I played the clarinet as a child. So, I am in the same band as you, playing my clarinet, okay?

We are going to play "Lift Every Voice and Sing". Just about everyone is playing beautifully, but one boy starts playing, "We Will Rock You," and a girl in the back starts playing, "Twinkle, Twinkle, Little Star".

Now, we all sound unprofessional because we are no longer harmonizing. The audience will leave the concert hall.

Likewise, we as humans are intended to be in harmony – with God, with each other, and with nature. How can we be in harmony with God? Through taking care of God's creations. God's creation that we are most intimate with on a daily basis is our own body. When we take care of our bodies, respect our bodies, and strengthen our bodies, we honor God.

We can take care of each other by being nice to each other,

being supportive of each other, nurturing the sick, assisting the elderly, and feeding the hungry.

Thirdly, I mentioned being in harmony with nature. We can be in harmony with nature by making a vow to never litter, by recycling or re-using our trash, by gardening and planting trees, and by making use of natural renewable energy sources such as solar and wind power.

Also, to be in harmony with nature, we can create new technologies that improve or maintain the environment, rather than destroying it. For example, we could invent a form of transportation that runs off water instead of fossil fuel and does not emit any toxic smoke.

BALANCE – Balance is one of the most important principles to apply to our everyday lives. Balance is defined as, "an even distribution of weight enabling someone or something to remain upright and steady."

As a young student, you have to balance your schoolwork, your extracurricular activities, and your social life with friends while also maintaining good relationships with your family members, eating a good diet, exercising, and keeping a positive attitude.

When you become an adult, you will have to balance working or running your business and taking care of your family along with everything else.

Some students lose balance by spending too much time with friends and not enough time on schoolwork. Others lose balance by doing well in school, but eating a poor diet and not exercising.

We want to always strive for health in every area of our lives - healthy grades, healthy relationships, a healthy mind, and a healthy body. Always seek balance.

ORDER – Order is the arrangement of people or things in relation to each other. According to ancient African knowledge, God comes first, then the angels and the ancestors, then humans, then animals, then inanimate objects like rocks and water[4].

Thus, each level on this hierarchy strives to be in harmony with all other levels while taking care of the levels beneath one's level. God takes care of everything, the angels and the ancestors serve

---

[4] See *Muntu: African Culture and the Western World* by Jahnheinz Jahn.

humanity, and humans must take care of the animals and the earth.

Likewise, there is a hierarchy within humanity. When we are young, we listen to our parents and other elders, because they are older and wiser. They generally want the best for us. Similarly, when we become parents and elders, we guide our children and seek to improve our communities.

RECIPROCITY – To practice reciprocity is to act in ways that are mutually beneficial to all parties involved. For example, we want others to be nice to us, so we must also be nice to others.

However, if you are being nice to someone and they are being mean, distance yourself from that person, if possible. He or she is not practicing reciprocity. People who make a habit of not practicing reciprocity are not people who you want as friends.

We should seek to establish reciprocity in all of our relationships. Your parents take good care of you, work to give you the best education, and secure money to make sure that you have food, clothing, and shelter. Thus, you should also find ways to help your parents.

You can assist your parents by making extra efforts to do chores without being asked, by being a good student, by being respectful, and by being considerate.

PROPRIETY - Propriety is the condition of being right, appropriate or fitting. Synonyms of propriety are decency, courtesy, and modesty. In other words, we want to understand the settings that we are in and act appropriately.

For example, if you are at school/homeschool, know that it is time for education and act appropriately. If you are at church, the mosque, or the Ile, it is not time to play; it is time to act fittingly in that spiritual setting. If you are hanging out with your friends, still behave in a way that reflects what your parents have taught you and general respect for yourself.

When you practice propriety, you do not need someone to always watch you or tell you what is right and wrong because you know right from wrong and live it independently. You also know that if you make a mistake, you seek to learn your lesson and not make that same mistake again.

Many children, maybe some you know, act one way when adults

are watching and another way when they are with friends. These children are behaving on an animalistic level – as if they need a leash to behave in a suitable way. When you practice propriety, you are behaving as a human being with self-discipline, willpower, and good character.

ACTIVITIES:

1. Give oral or written examples of how you can practice each of the seven principles of Ma'at.
2. If you had to choose an eighth principle of Ma'at, what would it be?

3. Use the internet to research an African American or African leader and write three paragraphs about how they practiced one or more of the principles of Ma'at.

4. Write a 1 – 2 page skit about the practice of one of the principles of Ma'at.

THE 42 ADMONITIONS OF MA'AT

There are also 42 admonitions associated with Ma'at. An admonition tells you what to avoid. It warns you against something. In the Bible, you see admonitions in the form of the 10 commandments. In

Kemet, there were 42 admonitions instead of 10. Notice that instead of saying, "thou shalt not," these admonitions say, "I have not". That means that when you read them aloud, you are testifying to what you have and have not done. If you say that you have not done something that you really did do, then you would be lying and no one wants to be a liar. Let's read 33 of the 42 admonitions of Ma'at and then create our own admonitions.

1) I have not committed sin.
2) I have not stolen.
3) I have not slain men or women.
4) I have not stolen food.
5) I have not swindled offerings.

6) I have not stolen from God/Goddess.

7) I have not told lies.

8) I have not carried away food.

9) I have not cursed.

10) I have not closed my ears to truth.

11) I have not made anyone cry.

12) I have not felt sorrow without reason.

13) I have not assaulted anyone.

14) I am not deceitful.

15) I have not stolen anyone's land.

16) I have not been an eavesdropper.

17) I have not falsely accused anyone.

18) I have not been angry without reason.

19) I have not polluted myself.

20) I have not terrorized anyone.

21) I have not disobeyed the Law.

22) I have not been exclusively angry.

23) I have not behaved with violence.

24) I have not caused disruption of peace.

25) I have not acted hastily or without thought.

26) I have not exaggerated my words when speaking.

27) I have not used evil thoughts, words or deeds.

28) I have not polluted the water.

29) I have not spoken angrily or arrogantly.

30) I have not cursed anyone in thought, word or deeds.

31) I have not placed myself on a pedestal.

32) I have not stolen from or disrespected the deceased.

33) I have not taken food from a child.

These admonitions were written thousands of years ago to reflect the culture, geographical area, and time period, but many are still applicable to our lives today. Discuss with your teacher which admonitions you think best fit that time period and which ones that you feel are useful today.

ACTIVITIES:

1. Write 10 or more admonitions that you feel are relevant to your life today. Write them in the form, "I have not..." At the end of each day, say these admonitions aloud. If you actually did do something that is on your "I have not" list, skip that one, but make it a point to not do it the next day. This is a great character building exercise.

Examples:

- I have not disrespected my parents.

- I have not allowed myself to be pressured into wrongdoing.
- I have not overeaten.
- I have not lost my temper.

_____

_____

_____

_____

_____

_____

_____

_____

_____

_____

_____

_____

_____

2. Write a 16 line poem or 16 bar rap
   about the admonitions of Ma'at.

   Example:

   I have not stolen / because I
   love my brothers / I have not
   slain / because we take care of
   each other / I have not
   polluted / I take care of the
   earth / I have not spoken out of
   anger / because peace comes
   first...

_____

_____

3. Look up the Bible's 10
   Commandments and write 3
   paragraphs comparing and
   contrasting the 10
   Commandments to the 42
   Admonitions of Ma'at. First, use
   the Venn Diagram to brainstorm
   (see next page).

VENN DIAGRAM

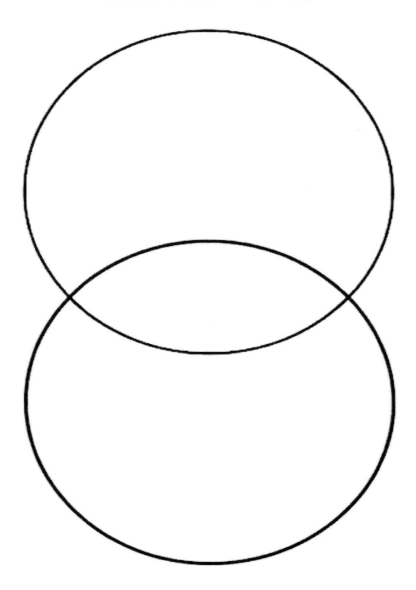

IWA PELE

"It is gentle character which enables the rope of life to remain strong in our hands." - Odu 119:1, *Odu Ifa*

Iwa Pele is Yoruba for good and gentle character. Yoruba is a language spoken in Nigeria[5], West Africa. The Yoruba people traditionally practiced Ifa, a spiritual system that honors God, the ancestors, and nature. One of the

---

[5] By US Gov [Public domain], via Wikimedia Commons

major goals of practicing Ifa is to develop and maintain Iwa Pele.

Let's examine some Yoruba proverbs[6] to see how they discuss Iwa Pele.

A kì í dá ọwọ́ lé ohun tí a ò lè gbé.

One does not lay one's hands on a load one cannot lift.

(One should not overreach.)

This proverb can be practiced through understanding what you can realistically do, and then doing that. For example, if you attempt to carry a thing that you know is too

---

[6] Proverbs documented at http://yoruba.unl.edu/yoruba-1.php.htm.

heavy for you, you may hurt yourself or break the thing.

Likewise, if you plan to do more in a day than you can realistically accomplish, there will not be good results. An example of this is cramming for a test. If you have a big test coming up, study for it little by little. It is not wise to try to memorize everything the night before the test.

A kì í fi pàtàkì bẹ́ èlùbọ́; ẹní bá níṣu ló m̄bẹ́ ẹ.

One does not come by yam-flour because of one's importance; only people who have yams can make yam flour.

(One cannot eat one's importance.)

One may be super popular or talented, but that does not mean anything on its own. How do we use our influence and talent? Some young people are praised so much on how smart they are or on their accomplishments that when they get older, they think that simply possessing these gifts makes them better than others. So, they don't work as hard as others and end up making poor grades or having no money.

Do you know someone who thinks they are so smart or cool, but they're always broke or making bad grades? A part of having good character is knowing that you actually have to do the work, consistently, to live the life that you want to live.

A kì í pèlú ọbọ jáko.

One does not join a monkey in roaming the bush.

(Do not join others in their madness.)

If some of your friends want to go do something that you know isn't right, that doesn't mean that you have to do it. Do you go to the zoo and start acting like the monkeys?

Sometimes, people can be monkeys too – through their

behavior. This also applies to when someone wants to fight or argue and you know that their actions do not make sense. If you start arguing back or fighting with them, you are engaging in that monkey behavior.

A kì í yàgò fún ẹlẹ́ṣin àná.

One does not get out of the way for a person who rode a horse yesterday.

(Past glory avails little in the present.)

Have you ever heard someone bragging about what they used to do or used to be? That doesn't matter in the present. If you plant a beautiful garden and then eat the food from it, the food is gone. You can't feed anyone off the harvest that was eaten last year. We have to plant new seeds.

We can learn from this proverb to always improve ourselves, to always do the work necessary, so that we can continually eat of the fruit of the seeds that we have planted.

À-jẹ-tán, à-jẹ-ì-mọra, ká fi ọwọ́ mẹ́wẹ̀ẹ̀wá jẹun ò yẹ ọmọ èèyàn.

Eating-absolutely-everything, eating-with-abandon, eating with all ten fingers is unworthy of human beings.

(People should not be slaves to food.)

This proverb is truly self-explanatory. We should eat to live, not live to eat. If we are eating too many unhealthy foods, overeating, or being so greedy that we will not share food – we are behaving like wild animals and not like human beings.

Food is meant to nourish and energize the body – not to be used just for pleasure or escape. Study good nutrition and practice it.

Àpárá ńlá, ìjà ní ńdà.

Excessive ribbing unfailingly leads to a fight.

(Jokes should know limits.)

Everyone likes to joke around, but joking carelessly can hurt other's feelings. We should always be considerate of how our words affect others. Do not joke at the expense of others.

For example, it's not okay to label others as too fat, too skinny, too short, too tall, too "light", too "dark", etc… There is no need to make fun of anyone's physical appearance.

God designed each person to be perfectly and uniquely beautiful. Likewise, it is bad character to put down others because of what they don't know or because they know quite a lot, i.e. calling someone "stupid" or "nerdy". Karma is real and what you do will come back around to you.

There are many other Yoruba proverbs that apply to every area of life. In West Africa, a person is considered wise by their ability to understand and apply proverbs without needing an explanation. The goal of following these proverbs and the goal of having good character is to become a good person.

When you are a good person, more good things will happen to you. You will live with greater ease, you will have more friends, you will have more money, and you will have more security. More people will want to be supportive of you, so you will have a better life.

But one important thing to remember – being a good person is just as much about helping yourself as it is about helping others. If you are always helping others and neglecting yourself – that is unwise behavior. Being a good person is about being wise and acting with good character.

ACTIVITIES:

1. Write 5 proverbs of your own that encourage good

character. Also, write their meanings.

Example:

- One can win more friends with a smile than with a frown.

  Meaning: If you have a positive attitude, you will have more friends.

_____

_____

_____

_____

_____

2. Draw a picture illustrating one of the Yoruba proverbs or one of your own.

3. Use the internet to find a proverb from another culture in Africa, Europe, or the Americas that has a similar meaning to one of the Yoruba proverbs listed above or to one of your own. Write it down here.

_____

_____

_____

_____

_____

_____

_____

NGUZO SABA

"Sticks in a bundle are unbreakable." ~Kenyan Proverb

 The *Nguzo Saba* (Swahili for Seven Principles) is a character-guiding system based on East African tenets. It was adapted in the 20th century by Maulana Karenga, an African American scholar into seven simple principles. These principles are the foundation of the African American holiday, Kwanzaa. During Kwanzaa (December 26 –

January 1 of each year), one strives to put the principles into practice on each of the seven days.

While Kwanzaa is the time that people most associate with the Nguzo Saba, it truly offers us guidance for the whole year round. Let's examine the Seven Principles, their meanings, and their practical applications.

UMOJA means unity.

KUJICHAGULIA means self-determination.

UJIMA means working together.

UJAMAA means supporting each other economically.

NIA means purpose.

KUUMBA means creativity.

IMANI means faith, especially faith in ourselves.

How can we practice these principles?

UMOJA: We can practice Umoja through acting in unity. If your family is trying to save money, it is not the time to ask for new sneakers or for a new gaming system. It would be wiser to think about how you can help them to save money. Your family's success is your success too.

Similarly, if your friend is trying to study for a big test, is it unwise to ask him or her to go to the movies. Offer to help your friend study instead.

KUJICHAGULIA: We can practice Self-Determination through taking actions that demonstrate our intelligence and strength. For example, if you are an athlete, you may at some point sprain a muscle. You can let that discourage you or you can take the necessary actions to heal properly, restore your muscle, and get back in the game!

Another example: If you want to buy something really cool, but you don't have enough money, you can start a business and save up to get what you want. You don't have to sit around waiting on your parents to give you everything – you can utilize Kujichagulia!

UJIMA: You can practice Ujima by remembering that we can accomplish more together than we can individually. If you have to paint a room, get a friend to help. If your friend has to paint a room, help your friend.

If you want to sell lemonade to fundraise for a cause, talk with 5 or

10 friends and set up stands on each block so that you can multiply the amount that you raise. Think about life like basketball – no matter how good you are, you can always score more points as a well-coordinated team.

UJAMAA: Ujamaa means cooperative economics. Always strive to support the people and the businesses that will keep our communities strong.

In Nigeria, groups of people put their money together to make large purchases or help someone in an emergency. Pooling your money together in Nigeria is called an Esusu.

African American communities could also become stronger through cooperative economics. If you want to purchase a gaming system that costs $400, could both you and your best friend put in $200 each and share it? Likewise, you two could put your money together and start a profitable business.

We must support each other. Search online to find the Black businesses in your area and begin buying your food, clothing, toys, and anything else that you can from these shops.

NIA: To practice Nia, we must try to find our purpose and live it. Also, we must do things with purpose – or meaning. If you are very gifted in certain areas, this is an indication that your purpose also involves these gifts.

You don't have to know your purpose right now, but work on bettering the talents with which you have been blessed so that you will be ready when you realize your purpose.

As far as doing things with meaning – here is an example. If you see a group of kids throwing eggs at a house, ask yourself, what is the purpose of them doing that? They are probably just bored.

If you join them, you will get in trouble with them. Instead, ask them, "What purpose does this serve?" You will find that they cannot give you a good answer.

Always ask yourself before taking any actions, "What purpose does this serve?" If you can't come up with a logical answer, don't do it.

KUUMBA: We can practice Kuumba by nurturing our creativity. If you like drawing, draw everyday so that you can become better at drawing. You will find great satisfaction in it, and if you choose to, you can use it to support yourself financially as an adult. This is true for anything that you really enjoy doing.

If you like painting, do it as much as possible. Take classes. Become your best. If you like football, play it as often as possible. What you water, grows. What you feed, grows. If you water and feed the creative gifts that you have been blessed with, they will grow.

IMANI: We can practice Imani by having faith in ourselves and having faith in our success. One of my good friends always says, "The superhero always wins in the ends." When you read comic books or watch cartoons, you see that the hero always triumphs.

You are the hero in your life. Even if you have a bad day or do poorly at a task, it will get better. If you have a goal, plan it out and go for it. Nine times out of ten, you will succeed. If you fail, try again. When your faith is unshakeable, you will have no worries because you know that things will always eventually work out in your favor.

You can also help this process by practicing good character. If you want to succeed at something that will hurt someone else, you will not succeed. Even if it seems like you're successful at first, you will ultimately fail if your intent is to hurt someone else with your success.

For example, let's say that you want to sell lemonade and your neighbor wants to sell lemonade, so you start telling people that your neighbor's lemonade has bugs in it. Maybe more people will buy your lemonade at first, but when they find out that you are not telling the truth, no one will support you.

Instead, you can practice unity with your neighbor and open one big lemonade stand. Or, you can offer strawberry lemonade instead of regular lemonade. That way, you can both be successful.

ACTIVITIES:

1. Write a short story 1 – 2 pages long about a person who practices all seven of the Nguzo Saba.

2. Write a plan for how you will implement each of the seven principles this year. One to two sentences for each principle is sufficient.

_____

_____

_____

_____

_____

_____

_____

_____

_____

_____

_____

_____

_____

3. Use the internet to find a song that represents one of the Nguzo Saba. Write the title and artist here.

ADINKRA SYMBOLS

The *Adinkra Symbols*[7] of Ghana, West Africa, are visual representations of characteristics or proverbs that relate to good character. These symbols, created by the Akan people, are often portrayed on fabrics, on carvings, on pottery, or on jewelry. Each time that a person sees the symbol, it reminds him or her to practice the meaning. Let's look at some of the Adinkra symbols and their meanings.

---

[7] See all Adinkra symbols at http://www.adinkra.org/

Adinkrahene:

Greatness, leadership

Akofena:

Courage, valor,

heroism

Akoma: Patience,

tolerance

Ananse Ntontan:
Wisdom,
Creativity

**Nea Onnim No
Sua A, Ohu**:
Symbol of
knowledge and
lifelong education

Sankofa: Learn from the past.

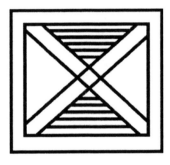

Mframadan: Fortitude and readiness.

Boa me na me mmoa wo: Help me and let me help you.

Aya: Endurance, resourcefulness

Sesa wo suban: Transform your character, transform your life.

What do you think is the significance of having symbols as reminders? As you think about this question, think of all the symbols that you see day to day as reminders. For example, when you see a red hexagon, it reminds you to stop. When you see the flag of your country, each color signifies a principle or concept that its founders valued.

Likewise, the Adinkra symbols resonate with the values of the Akan people and remind Ghanaians to embody these principles daily. If you had to create a new Adinkra symbol, what would it look like and what would it represent?

ACTIVITIES:

1. Make up your own Adinkra symbol. Draw a picture of it and write its meaning.

2. Draw a pattern of your favorite Adinkra symbols using crayons, markers, or paint on paper or cloth. Use lots of color!

3. Use fabric markers or fabric paint to draw an Adinkra symbol on a blank tee shirt. Wear it or sell it.

CHARACTER BUILDING EXAMPLES

CHARACTER BUILDING EXAMPLES

"You may fill your heads with knowledge or skillfully train your hands, but unless it is based upon high, upright character, upon a true heart, it will amount to nothing." - Booker T. Washington

QUEEN NZINGA

Queen Nzinga of Angola led her people in battle against the Portuguese. The Portuguese wanted to abuse her land and her people, but Queen Nzinga was brave enough to fight against them. She demonstrated **Justice** and **Self-Determination (Kujichagulia).**

SHAKA ZULU

Shaka Zulu was a great king and military leader in South Africa. Though he was born in a small chiefdom that was not considered very important, Shaka developed his intelligence, wisdom, and strength to become one of the greatest kings in history. He was also a military genius who won many battles. He was also known to be very encouraging and a great listener. King Shaka Zulu practiced **Balance** in being both a king and a military leader. He also utilized **Unity (Umoja)** and **Working Together (Ujima)** to lead his army and people.

MARCUS GARVEY

Marcus Garvey[8] was born in Jamaica in 1887 to a family of 11 children. He was the youngest. He read often as a child and began working as a teenager. In this way, he gained

---

[8] By from George Grantham Bain Collection [Public domain], via Wikimedia Commons

both knowledge and skill. By the age of 20, he started an organization to help African people around the world – the UNIA. He traveled to the United States and helped many African Americans to be proud of who they are, learn self-defense, start businesses, and reconnect with Africa. By the age of 22, he started his own naval shipping line to import and export between the United States, Africa, and the Caribbean. Marcus Garvey practiced **Ujamaa (Cooperative Economics)** through helping others become financially successful.

FANNIE LOU HAMER

Fannie Lou Hamer[9] was a civil rights activist born in 1917. When it was violently discouraged for African Americans in the South to vote, she risked her life for everyone to maintain their right to a democratic voice. While she was helping others vote, she was beaten and even shot, but she persevered. She demonstrated **Imani (Faith)** and a love for **Justice** through never giving up and always fighting for what was right.

---

[9] By Warren K. Leffler, U.S. News & World Report Magazine [Public domain], via Wikimedia Commons

ALICE WALKER

Alice Walker grew up poor. Her childhood was made harder when she was shot in the eye accidentally with a BB gun. She was ashamed of the scar left on her eye, so she spent a lot of time alone. She found happiness through reading and writing. Alice became a very good student. As a result, she received a scholarship for college and opportunities to travel to other countries. Using her experiences and her imagination, she began writing poetry and novels that became very popular. Along the way, Alice used her writing fame as way to promote peace and justice. Alice practiced **Propriety** through choosing to use her fame at the right times to advance **Harmony** in the world.

PUTTING PRINCIPLES INTO PRACTICE

PUTTING PRINCIPLES INTO PRACTICE

Below are extensions to continue putting the principles that you have learned into practice. Feel free to write in the "My Notes" section of this book, or use a separate notebook for the written exercises. Enjoy!

Creative Writing

1) Write a letter to your future self, telling him or her how to practice good character as an adult.

2) Write a short story about a boy or girl who does not have good character and the troubles that happen as a result.

3) Write a folktale about an animal that practices poor character and what happens because of this. Write a moral at the end of the story.

Music

1) Write a song about how one can practice good character.

2) Make up a dance about 5 principles that you learned in this book. For example, Self Determination can be pumping your fists in the air and stomping. Unity could

be clasping your hands
together.

3) Find 3 songs by activist
musicians such Stevie
Wonder, Gil Scott Heron,
Sweet Honey in the Rock,
Lauryn Hill, or Talib Kweli and
listen to the lyrics. Discuss.

Visual Art

1) Find the Adinkra Symbols
online and discuss their
meanings. Draw your
favorite Adinkra symbols on
a poster board and
decorate them with your
favorite colors.

2) Purchase fabric markers and a blank tee shirt. Design a shirt symbolizing one of the principles that you learned. Wear it or sell it.

3) Use printer paper or cardstock paper - folded in half – and markers, colored pencils, crayons, or paint to make a greeting card about one or more of the principles that you learned. Give it away or sell it.

Technology

1) Use the internet to research proverbs from at least 5 countries and discuss.

2) Use the internet to find where the Kemetic (Egypt), Yoruba (Nigeria), and Swahili (Kenya/Tanzania) live. Draw these countries on a separate sheet of paper. Write one principle from their tradition inside of the respective country.

Critical Thinking

1) Why do you think that it is important for societies to give people proverbs or laws that tell them how to practice good character?
2) What do you think would happen if people had no

laws or guidelines to tell
them right from wrong?

3) If you had to create your
own society, and you could
only have 5 rules, what
would they be?

COMMUNITY SERVICE EXTENSIONS

It is important that we put the
character building principles that we
learned into action in our
communities. Choose three or more
items from the list below to begin
working on immediately.

THINGS WE CAN DO TO MAKE OUR COMMUNITIES BETTER[10]

---

[10] From *Tomorrow Will be Better* by Nikala Asante

- Be good to each other.
- Feed the homeless.
- Pick up trash.
- Start a community garden or volunteer with one that already exists.
- Study, promote, and practice good nutrition, self-care, and fitness.
- Mentor.
- Take parenting classes if you plan to be a parent one day. Better parents make a better world.
- Take or teach self-defense classes. Strong people make strong communities.
- Attend financial literacy and/or entrepreneurial workshops. Healthy finances are a part of a healthy community.
- Tutor a struggling student.
- Study the history of your culture. If we know where we came from, we will have a better sense of where we're going.

- Cook a meal for an elder once per week.
- Write a letter or send a book to someone in prison.
- Babysit one night a month free for a single parent.
- Start or join your neighborhood watch.
- Smile, give hugs, and say "I love you".

MY GLOSSARY

Write all of the new words that you read in this book here. Look them up in the dictionary and write a short definition for each word.

_____

_____

_____

_____

_____

_____

_____

_____

_____

MY NOTES

SPECIAL ACKNOWLEDGEMENTS

I would first of all like to give thanks to the Creator for allowing me to engage in purposeful life work. Special thanks to Deirdre Mimes Danner for being supportive and inspirational from the beginning.

Thank you to Deloyd Parker of the S.H.A.P.E. Community Center, Baba Shango of SEHAH Youth and Fitness, Dr. James Conyers and Dr. Malachi Crawford of the University of Houston African American Studies Program, Mama Tracy and Mama Judy of New World Learning Institute, Mama Imani and Mama Lola of Sisterhood Creations, and Sister Hamdiyah Ali of Project Row Houses for your support and love along this path. Thank you for granting me opportunities to teach and learn, mentorship, and guidance!

Thank you to my beautiful parents and my amazing son for your love and support each day. Truly, there is no me without you.

Thank you to my brothers in the scholar-warrior work who inspire me each day – Asar Imhotep, Dr. Samori Camara, and Dr. Sujan Dass. Thank you to my sisters who have been supportive of my homeschooling journey – Nzinga and Het-Hru.

Thank you to my homeschooling family in Houston. Anyone who I have failed to mention, please charge it to my head and not my heart. I love you all and I am very appreciative.

Asante Sana!

With Love,

Nikala Asante

ABOUT THE AUTHOR

Nikala Asante is a mother, scholar, creative writer, independent educator, and international Human Rights advocate from Houston, TX. She is an alumni of the University of Houston Honors College, holding a BA in English Creative Writing with a minor in Africana Studies. She has traversed 8 countries outside of the United States engaging in research and service projects which inform her knowledge and passion for Africana Studies and Human Rights.

Within her community, Asante organizes homeschooling parents around educational events and field trips to advance their children's learning experiences, as well as tutoring and mentoring youth.

In the realm of Human Rights, Asante has traveled to Dominican Republic and Haiti regularly since 2013 with established organizations and independently to raise awareness about injustices in the garment industry, to help set up and manage pop-up medical clinics, to distribute food, water, and supplies, to plant food bearing trees in deforested areas, and to assist in creating archives of personal narratives about Haiti's 2010 earthquake.

Asante has received numerous awards from the community and university, including the prestigious Gilman International Study Scholarship. She was featured in Defender Networks' Black History special on young leaders, "Following in the Footsteps of Dr. Martin Luther King, Jr." in 2013, on PBS *NewsHour* in 2015, and has spoken on Human Rights in two documentaries ("16th Strike: the Documentary" and "Nice: A Place to Start").

Additionally, Asante has published two collections of poetry and short stories, *Graffiti*

Nommo and *Re-Divining Self* and one non-fiction social justice primer for youth, *Tomorrow Will Be Better*. Further, in 2014, she wrote and produced her first episodic web series for youth empowerment, "Pharaoh the Web Series", a satire addressing problems young African American males face in American society. "Pharaoh" was filmed and directed by Derek Michael Parker. It is available for viewing on YouTube.

Asante's social commentary, poetry, and short stories have also been featured in notable print publications and anthologies such as *Tre Magazine, The Houston Sun, Black Science Fiction Society's Genesis Anthology Book II, and Genesis Science Fiction Magazine.*

As a professional Spoken Word artist, Asante has read and performed her poetry locally, nationally, and internationally. Asante is available for booking for public speaking engagements, educational workshops, Spoken Word performances, and book signings.

Websites:

nikalaasante.com

blackhomeschoolmom.com

asanteglobalworks.com

For booking, please contact through blackhomeschoolmom.com.